ANNEKE WILLS
in focus: a life in images

Anneke Wills
& Paul W.T. Ballard

fantom
publishing

"For all my dear friends in the wonderful
world of Doctor Who.

In deep gratitude."

"It is curious to look at a photo
of oneself when you are one and a half
and to think that same spirit is still
with you today.
Magic. I haven't really changed at all!"
ANNEKE

"I got paid £9 for the film: my first wage packet! I was very proud to present it to my mother."
ANNEKE

Radio Times (Incorporating World-Radio) March 1, 1957. Vol. 134: No. 1738.

MARCH 3—9

TELEVISION BBC AND SOUND
RADIO TIMES
PRICE THREEPENCE

'The Railway Children'

Meet them and their friend the station-master in Children's Television on Sunday,
when the famous story by E. Nesbit starts as a serial play for all the family

THE JILL DAY SHOW   ★   TED HEATH IS BACK
Thursday, Television (see page 9)   Tuesday, Light (see page 9)

FOR THE CHILDREN

The Railway Children: (l. to r.) Sandra Michaels as Phyllis, Anneke Willys as Roberta, and Cavan Kendall as Peter

A Railway and a Family

IN 1951 I produced a dramatised version of Mrs. Nesbit's book called *The Railway Children*. It was actually the second serial we presented on Children's Television and now almost a new generation of children has grown up apart from the countless families who were not able to see television in those days. You can see the first part on Sunday. So it seems the right moment to produce it again.

This is a story for all ages and for both sexes and although the railway itself—with Perks, the porter, Mr. Gill the stationmaster, and the Old Gentleman—becomes so dear to the three children, Roberta, Peter, and Phyllis, it is not a book about Railways. It is about a family—who have their exciting times, their sad times, birthdays, illnesses, and accidents just like any family who might be looking in today.

Half the charm of Mrs. Nesbit's books—and their names are as familiar today as when they were first written—*The Treasure Seekers*, *The Would-be-Goods*, *Five Children and It*, and so many more—lies in their Early Edwardian atmosphere. Those were the days when boys wore knickerbocker suits and the girls pinafores and red flannel petticoats—petticoats which were to prove so enormously valuable to the children and to the train on one momentous occasion.

Filming in 1957 for the period of 1906 means finding a station and a bit of line that is not electrified. After quite a long search—walking on remote bits of line in the home counties and consulting ordnance maps, we have found a country station and a line that winds through a tunnel between high wooded hills—but there are difficulties involved in that there are also modern trains running their day-to-day schedule. However, thanks to the great co-operation we have received from British Railways we hope we shall manage to get all the shots we want without any keen trainspotters feeling compelled to write us critical letters.

DOROTHEA BROOKING

"The production team took great care to get the period details right and were most upset when the BBC photographer for Radio Times took a shot showing a modern signal box and white line painted for blackouts during the war."
ANNEKE

"I was dismissed from RADA... I think I pushed them too far with my rebellious streak!"
ANNEKE

"My passport photo!"
ANNEKE

"Anneke and I have more than
Doctor Who in common - among other
things we also share a love of
gardening and champagne.
But whether we are immersing
ourselves in Daleks, Delphiniums or
Dom Perignon, she is always the
finest of companions."
NICHOLAS PEGG

"Our eyes met. And love happened."
ANNEKE

"The wonderful series Gurney Slade.
Notoriously ahead of its time."
ANNEKE

"I had a real Sixties look that the BBC loved."
ANNEKE

"There was a scene in Some People
where I shrink my jeans in the bath.
At the premiere, the Duke of Edinburgh asked me
if it really worked, and I replied cheekily
"Yeah, you should try it!"
ANNEKE

"I can date The Sentimental Agent
immediately... because I remember the boots!"
ANNEKE

"One of the groundbreaking Plays Of The Week.
My character is sending Richard Vernon crazy in her
leather miniskirt."
ANNEKE

I Marion Mathie and Annika Wills *The Primitive* means a big break. Neither has before had the chance to play a strong, emotional, down-to-earth role on television.

In this play by Anthony Couch they are cast as mother and daughter.

The story centres on the return home of Dave Short (Stephen Lewis) after serving eight-and-a-half years in prison for robbery with violence.

Marion Mathie plays May, Dave's wife, who has fallen in love with her lodger, Robert (Scott Forbes), an advertising executive. Dave's return May plans to leave her husband, but to avoid spoiling his first days of freedom, she postpones telling him the truth.

Dave's daughter Kathleen (Annika Wills) was nine years old when she last saw her father. His arrest had a deep effect on her. Now she is anxious to be rid of him. She has agreed, however, to cover up for her mother by pretending that Robert is her fiancé.

Marion Mathie — made what she called "a long slog through repertory" before coming into television four years ago.

"Ever since then I've mainly been cast as brittle, snobbish, sophisticated characters," she said. "But I'd rather play a genuine feel..."

MAN RETURNS

The Primitive
Play of the Week
Tuesday 9.35 p.m.

...myself, and it maddens me." said Annika. "I'm natural, that's all. But I wear what's comfortable. But I conform when occasion demands!"

She looked down at her grey pullover, topping a grey, gathered skirt. Her long legs were bare, her feet in sandals. Nothing startlingly non-conformist there.

Her flaxen hair, worn long and straight (I have to work on it to keep it from curling) is set off by a golden tan acquired earlier this year in Spain.

Annika and her elder brother, a journalist, live on the top floor of a narrow, three-storey house in London. Two of their friends are installed on the first and second floors.

"One is a film cutter and the other paints and plays the flute," said Annika. "The kitchen is shared by all with Annika doing the...

...all confusion, but we lived...she said. "I lived...

...alone for a while, and the silence was terrible."

Stephen Lewis, of East London's Theatre Workshop, plays Dave. Lewis is also a writer, and in his fourth stage play *Sparrers Can't Sing*, there is also a discharged prisoner.

Anthony Couch, explaining the play's title, said: "Dave's optimism is a primitive emotion. He believes he can bury the past."

Sarah Snow

Stephen Lewis and Marion Mathie in *The Primitive* . . .

and Scott Forbes and Annika Wills in another scene from the play

13

9.30 WINNING WIDOWS
starring
PEGGY MOUNT
and
AVICE LANDON
with
DAVID STOLL
By Sid Green and Dick Hills

A young niece arrives unexpectedly and leads Mildred and Martha into the strange world of beat, beatniks and coffee bars

Cast:
Martha	Peggy Mount
Mildred	Avice Landon
Vicar	David Stoll
Waitress	Anne Carroll
Teddy	Robert Scroggins
Girl	Frances White
Flash	Paul Cole
Sheila	Anneke Wills

Music composed by Bob Sharples
Played by Jack Parnell's Orchestra
Designer Michael Eve
Directed by DICKY LEEMAN
Produced by ALAN TARRANT
ATV Network Production

● What's in a name?—Page 42

Anneke Wills in a scene from Winning Widows at 9.30, in which she plays the niece who arrives unexpectedly

Keep on Running

Smith and Anneke Wills are the stars of tonight's Thirty-Minute Theatre

WHEN George meets a nice dolly that takes his fancy he doesn't usually have much trouble. In fact he has never had much trouble. He got in and out of grammar school with equal ease. Then he took up house-painting. He reckons that is as good a job as anything. You won't catch him in an office.

But when he spies Julia through the haze of not-to-be-painting—his two minds whether or not to join the party, he is in two minds whether he might well. It is the school-effect air of unobtainability that gets other. He finally decides he might seek her air of unobtainability with the trouser-suits him. All these slick chicks with the trouser-suits and eyelashes are getting a bit boring.

George has an assortment of ploys which he tries more or less indiscriminately. One of them never fails to work. But this time he does need a kind of campaign. Maybe it's because she doesn't behave like other girls. Maybe, but she doesn't need such kinds of opposition. George, you've coped with it well.

This is Vickery Turner's first play. She is a young actress recently seen as Eileen in *Up the Junction*.

If you turn on tonight you may brush up your technique, build up your resistance, or merely discover just who does keep on running.

KENNETH TRODD

Scott Forbes (left) and Donald...

PLAY BILL by SARAH SNOW

Mr Bell's out of tune

ERIC PORTMAN, long established as a straight leading actor in films and the theatre, turned to character acting as an unsuccessful schoolmaster in Terence Rattigan's *The Browning Version*.

"I'd never played a character part," he said, "and I didn't think I could. But when Terence Rattigan persuaded me to play Crocker-Harris, my first middle-aged role, it turned out to be my first big success in London." That was in 1948. Portman has been showing his full range ever since—notably in *Separate Tables*, written for him by Rattigan. This ran for two years in America after its London run.

Now Portman appears in an ITV play, *The Different Drum* —again as an unsuccessful schoolmaster, Mr. Bell.

The Different... Television... Thursda...

...told me: ...mar school ...has dreamed ...ing great ...finds he is ...with them.

"To...must be...resent...artistic...conven...

But...ing a...in o...play...und...and...th...b...

Joyce Heron and Eric Portman as Mr. and Mrs. Bell

FULL (NUCL AHE

SUDDENLY a nuclear-powered liner increases speed on her maiden voyage; there is no apparent reason... *This is the dramatic theme of The... Couldn't Stop.*... as

...they had reached the heart of ...the powerful new ship. ...father Holland (Donald ...ained the ...of... down logically his...the ship...*The Crusader*...sult of join...

FOR seven years and 3,213 performances, audiences at a New York theatre laughed at *Life with Father*. It rocked audiences in London, too. This is the family play of all time.

Now Renee Asherson and Jack Gwillim star as Vinnie and Clarence Day in the Granada presentation of this successful comedy.

Howard Lindsay and Russell Crouse based the play on Clarence Day's sketches of his father, also called Clarence. When they wrote it, after the younger Day's death in 1935, they sought the help of the family.

Madison-avenue just before the turn of the century was the upper-bracket residential part of New York. There the Days —red hair predominating—led a happy family life, punctuated by alarms and confusions.

For charming, spirited Vinnie Day the revelation that her husband had never been christened was a shock. The eldest of her three sons was 17. Vinnie determined that her husband should be baptised at once. She won the bustling support of Dr. Lloyd, a minister played by Lloyd Pearson.

The distinguished, energetic Clarence Day has a stubborn streak. In most things his wife can manage him, but can she succeed here?

"He is the universal father everyone will recognise," said Jack Gwillim. "He can be outrageous, but his family can be exasperating."

David Brierley, a youthful... plays the 17-year-old son ...nce. He said: "Clarence ...aps—he develops a liking ...ly."

...e's country cousin Cora...

Jack Gwillim and Renee Asherson

The happy Days

Life with Father
Play of the Week
Tuesday 9.35 p.m.

(Suzanne Finlay) comes to stay, bringing with her a 17-year-old friend, Mary Skinner (Perlita Neilson). Their visit, kept secret from father Day until it is too late for him to do anything but accept the situation, adds fuel to the confusion.

Suzanne Finlay, the only American in the cast, appeared at rehearsals each day in a different pair of slacks.

"There has been some speculation about whether I can last out rehearsals without repeating myself," she said. "But I think I'll make it. I have a great many, all sorts and colours."

The second son, 15-year-old John, is played by 19-year-old Richard Palmer, and another Richard plays the 13-year-old youngest Day. Whitney. He is Richard Williams and he plays his own age.

Renee Asherson, whose part is a change from "the nervous, highly strung creatures I've usually played on television," sympathises with Vinnie about money.

David Brierley and Perlita Neilson

..husband over the housekeeping," said Renee. "Luckily, she has an instinctively feminine flair for managing her husband in these awkward situations."

Renee Asherson has never before played an American on television. The first time she needed a Transatlantic accent was in 1949 in *A Streetcar Named Desire*.

"The Sixties were a really innovative
time for drama."
ANNEKE

My Polly
sweet shining light —
how poignant that I should be
remembered by your name —
My heart
forever
broken.

"We were on our way to do
a tour of the United States and
the press took a picture of us.
When we got to New York I blew
everyone away as I was the first to
have thigh boots!"
ANNEKE

"The Avengers saw the new woman
emerging on screen...
assertive and equal to the men."
ANNEKE

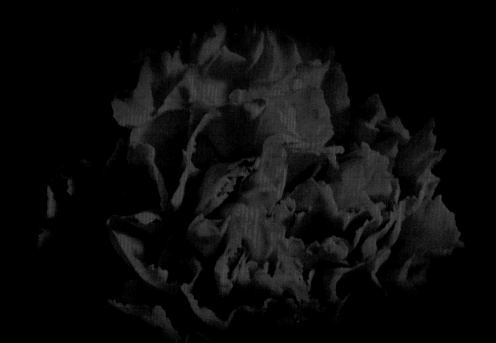

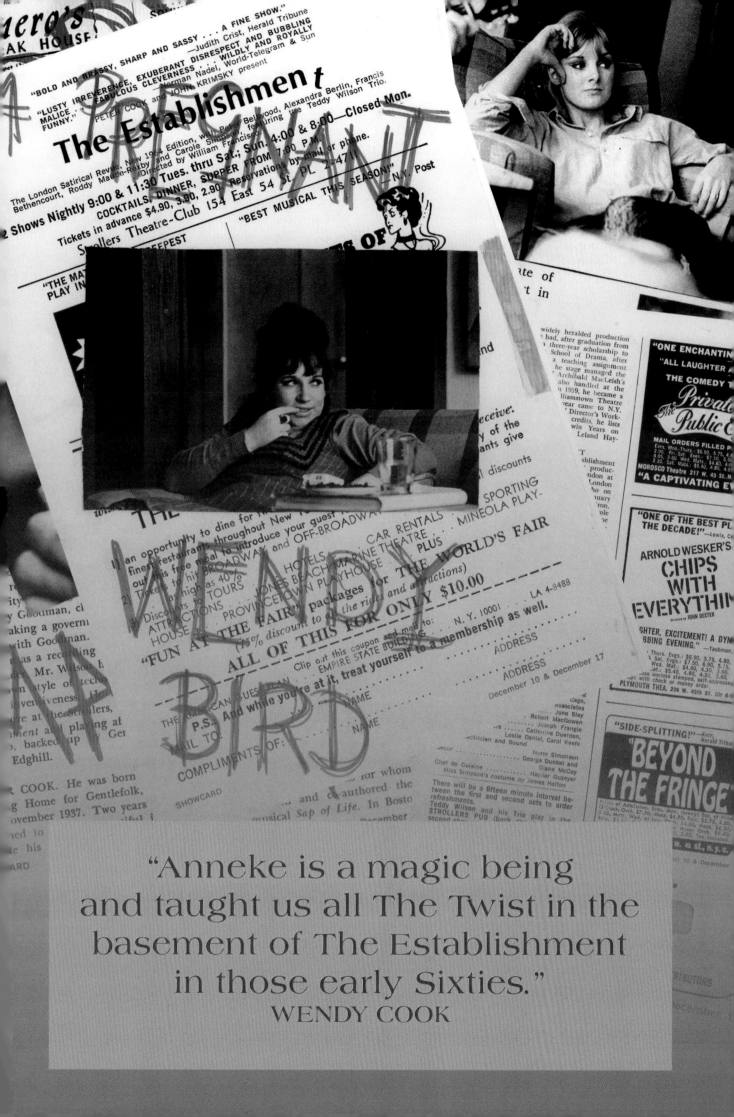

"Anneke is a magic being and taught us all The Twist in the basement of The Establishment in those early Sixties."
WENDY COOK

"I look at The Pleasure Girls now and
I think what's interesting is that it is telling the
story of a different London; there was a sort of
naivety to it all

We were all kind of naive really.
ANNEKE

KINEMATOGRAPH WEEKLY

APRIL 22, 1965   No. 3003
Vol. 575

Registered at the G.P.O.
as a Newspaper

PER ANNUM 118s. POST FREE
— HOME AND OVERSEAS —
SINGLE COPY 3s.

KINE WEEKLY

Bitter-sweet
Beauties of
Bed-sitter Land . . .

Michael Klinger and Tony Tenser present

THE PLEASURE GIRLS

Guest star

AN McSHANE   FRANCESCA ANNIS   KLAUS KINS

Co-starring MARK EDEN, TONY TANNER, SUZANNA LEIGH and Introducing ROSEMARY NICOLS

Produced by Harry Fine Written and directed by Gerry O'Hara

Compton-Cameo Films

60-62   OLD   COMPTON   STREET   LONDON

BRANCHES THROUGHOUT THE UNITE

7521

"With the lovely late Sir Roger Moore.
His nickname for me was "knickers" because
of my bloomers from Bloomingdales."
ANNEKE

"It was very different to the BBC. They bought me
the dress, the handbag and the shoes. The Beeb never
had the money for that... I was very pleased, this was
a proper costume!"
ANNEKE

Robin

my brother –

so crazy – so passionate

left us when you were 28

in circumstances that remain

unanswered –

forever with me in spirit

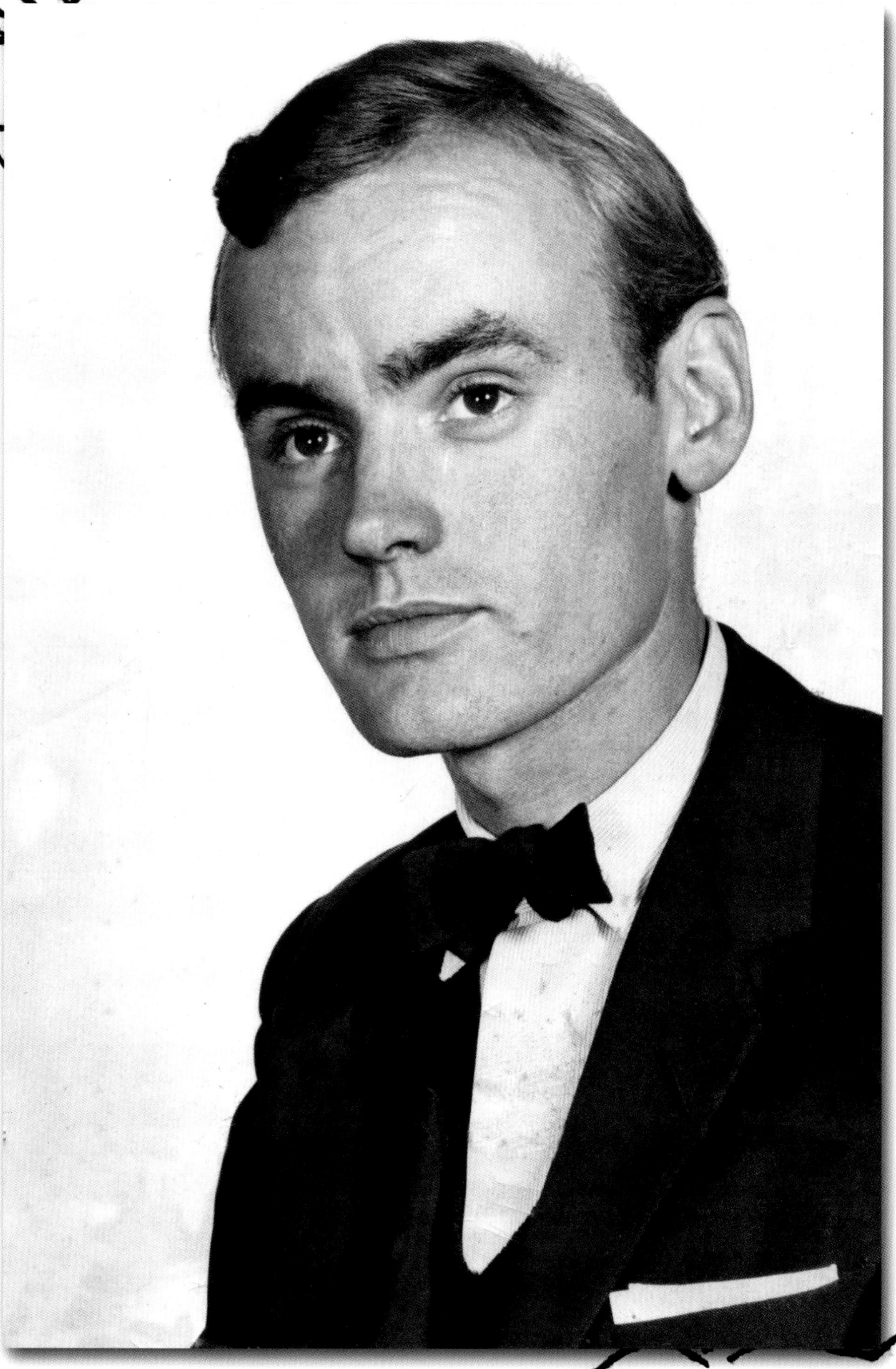

"Posing with Mickgough....
I'm pregnant with Jasper here."
ANNEKE

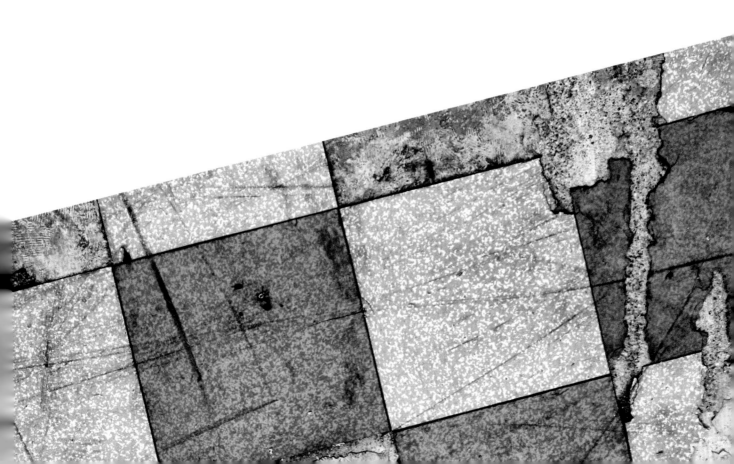

Lovely Anneke -
we have always known
her as "Wilks" -
since she was 19 -
a joyful ray of beauty,
sunshine and talent
in our lives!

— Evie &
Leslie Briaser

Polly.
24, private secretary to scientist.
Father, country doctor in Devon, four
brothers (one older - three younger).
Happy and conventional middle-class
background, she has never been tied
to her mother's apron strings - they
never know when to expect her home
but when she arrives they are happy
to see her. Has been, in turn, a travel
courier - done a small amount of
modelling (which she found irksome to
her intelligence and feet).

She loves sports cars, watching motor
racing, skiing, clothes, swimming - pet
hates: pomposity, deb's delights,
conforming and officials (police to
ticket collectors).

Intelligent, imaginative, impulsive,
inclined to act first, think later.
She is totally undomesticated,
cannot sew, knit or cook.

"We thought the audience
would identify with this leggy
swinging Sixties girl."
GERRY DAVIS

"I adored Patrick. What a gift
to be with him at that time. The
fact that his private life was in
total upheaval and the amount of
pressure he was under in those first
weeks as Doctor Who, it's utterly
astounding that he managed to be so
sweet, so kind, and
with so much humour.

That was the quality of the man."

ANNEKE

"Anneke was a complete child of her time...
and an excellent choice as the assistant."
CHRISTOPHER BARRY

"I got on very well with Anneke. We were great buddies.
We were great social animals... She was far more 'swinging'
than I was. She was raving it up the King's Road
with the Ozzy Clarkes and the Mary Quants and all that."
MICHAEL CRAZE

"Anneke is a true professional,
and a delight to work with.
She gives 100% to each reading she
does, and immerses herself in the spirit
of the piece.
She brings sunshine with her, and
brightens the day with her energy
and positivity."
MICHAEL STEVENS

"Family times."
ANNEKE

"My very own, very dear mum."
JASPER GOUGH

"Pre-filming on Strange Report, but the big question is…
'Who is in the limo behind me?'"
ANNEKE

"On the Southbank in London, shooting
the title sequence for Strange Report."
ANNEKE

"Tony Quayle was heavenly to work with on Strange Report
because he was so talented and mature. As a youngster you get better
working with people like that as it ups your game. Kaz Garas was
lovely too: I was privileged to be part of that team."
ANNEKE

"Quintessentially Sixties."
ANNEKE

"With the gorgeous Peter Cook at the premiere of Bedazzled."
ANNEKE

"Mickgough and I.
A love for lifetimes."
ANNEKE

"We all went to the Jolly Farmers pub opposite my home and the Cybermen had boiled eggs for breakfast!"
ANNEKE

"We lived, loved, danced and worked.
A special community creating
spiritually and artistically."
ANNEKE

"Cleaning houses in San Francisco!"
ANNEKE

"Meditating on life
in my bathtub on Hornby Island."
ANNEKE

"My pastels...
The Duchess and the sailor."
ANNEKE

"With my honest, forthright friend.
He will always be missed."
ANNEKE

"I have never worked with Anneke,
however I have had the pleasure of meeting
her many times at Doctor Who gigs.
She is warm, generous, kind and funny.
I will never forget her graphic description of
tantric sex!
It is a privilege to call her a friend."
WENDY PADBURY

"Anneke is an extraordinary human being
leading an extraordinary life.
She is a "once in a lifetime" person with whom
I have the great good fortune to be friends."
SOPHIE ALDRED

"Anneke is one of
those people who you are
glad to have in your life.
She's truly one of a kind.
I always look forward to
the next time I'll see
her at the studio or a
convention, and
we'll sit down and
natter for ages.
What a great part of
Doctor Who, and
a great person
to be around."
DAVID RICHARDSON

"I adore Anneke - she's been a constant in my Doctor Who experience from my first convention in 1998, right through to directing her in the Companion Chronicles.
She's warm, generous, caring and joyous and a lovely actress to boot!
Having Anneke around is always fun!
LISA BOWERMAN

"About a quarter of a century ago, I watched a fuzzy, hundredth-generation copy of 'The War Machines' and saw Polly and Ben in action for the first time. I was smitten!
I think what I really responded to about them was their sense of fun. You really felt that they enjoyed their adventures with the Doctor, and each other's company. I could hardly have imagined that, the next time Anneke Wills played the role of Polly, I would be writing it..."
STEVE LYONS

Amazing
Nutcase
Never shuts up
Elysian
Kinetic
Everlasting love

GARY RUSSELL

"One can only imagine the effect you've had on men over the decades, and you've still got it, kid!"

PATRICK MULKERN

"Still collecting Doctors!"
ANNEKE

Brains and beauty.
And she can write.
what's not to love?

Paul Wilson

"My favourite companion from
the new series.
A lovely actress with a great big heart."
ANNEKE

"When I first worked with Anneke we
were playing bisexual lizard creatures.
As we compared notes on reptilian hissing
and tongue-flicking,
I knew I'd found a friend for life."
BARNABY EDWARDS

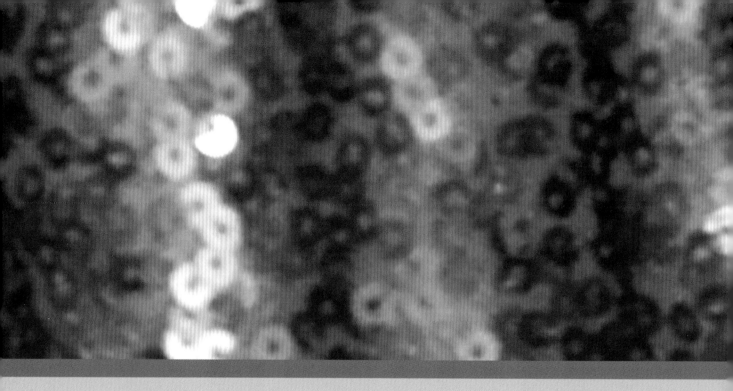

"Anneke is one of the most empathic, down-to-Earth, tactile, loving and compassionate people whom it has been my pleasure to meet. That said, if one was to be imprisoned with her (which isn't as unlikely as it sounds) she'd be the first to knock out the cruel guard, truss them up somewhere uncomfortable, and then lead a raid on the governor's drinks cabinet, giggling as she did it. And that's why I REALLY like her."

TOBY HADOKE

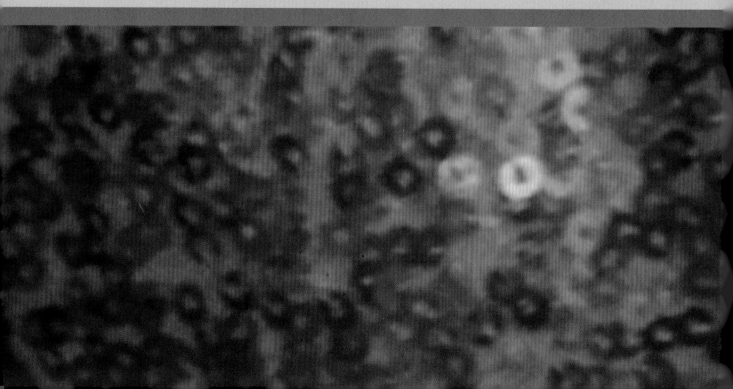

"To meet you once again, after half
a century, makes travelling through time
a real joy... With love."
DONALD VAN DER MAATEN

ACKNOWLEDGEMENTS

Anneke and the publishers would like to thank:
Stephen Aitkinson, Sophie Aldred, Christopher Barry, Lisa Bowerman, Yvonne & Leslie Bricusse, Michael Cole, Wendy Cook, Barnaby Edwards, Matt Evenden, Big Finish, Giles Golding, Jasper Gough, Toby Hadoke, Martin Herrison, Steve Lyons, Paul McGann, John Magee, Massimo Moretti, Patrick Mulkern, Carl Murphy, Wendy Padbury, Nicholas Pegg, Ben Preston, David Richardson, Gary Russell, Michael Stevens, Jonathan Talbot, Donald Van Der Maaten.

All images are from Anneke's personal archive, except for: (Cover, 3, 44, 57, 58, 60, 70, 71, 72, 73 © Michael Wallis Estate)
(8, 9, 92, 93 © Radio Times) (12, 13 © John Cole Estate) (17 © Jonathan Talbot)
(26, 27, 28, 29, 49, 50, 51, 78, 79, 85 © ITV/Rex Features) (42, 43 © Canal + Image UK) (64, 65 © Don Smith/Radio Times)
(66, 67 © Alexandra Tynan) (104, 105 © John Magee) (106, 107, 122, 125, 126 © Paul W.T. Ballard) (108, 109 © Lisa Bowerman)
(110 © David Richardson) (111 © Big Finish) (112, 113, 114, 115 © Dexter O'Neill) (116 (top), 117, 119 © Martin Herrison)
(116 (bottom) © Carl Murphy) (120 © GilesG Photography) (128 © Matt Evenden)
All quotes are directly from the individuals named, bar Gerry Davis and Michael Craze, which are sourced from
Doctor Who Magazine.
Every effort has been made to trace the copyright holders of the illustrative material herein. In the event we may have overlooked a clearance please contact the publisher so we can rectify this in future editions.

First published in hardback in 2012 by Fantom Films Ltd. This new edition first published in 2017.
www.fantomfilms.co.uk
© Anneke Wills and Paul W.T. Ballard 2017
A catalogue record of this book is available from the British Library.
ISBN: 978-1-78196-130-8
Printed by Instantprint Pro, Rotherham